Unconditional Boundaries

A Revolutionary Approach to Building Harmony and Authenticity In Relationships

Andy Lidstone

This book is dedicated to the people in my life who prove the concepts contained herein. To My friends Marleaux Flournoy, Leslie Gaudet and Leslie Shriner, without whom I would have never gotten this book finished. To my coach Michelle Moore who encouraged the original concepts. To the proliferation of other coaches who've journeyed with me and helped me in so many ways as I navigated my own trials. All of you have helped me test, refine, and prove the concepts and ideas that make up the backbone of this book. And a big thank you to my family. I love you all.

CONTENTS

Forward

As I look back on my life, I can clearly see the trials and tribulations that led me towards the fundamental discovery that forms the core of this book. The journey I embarked upon was a deeply personal exploration from the depths of isolation to the pinnacles of connection. It's a journey that started from a position of immense loneliness in my childhood, transitioned into a phase of persistent people-pleasing as a teenager and young adult, passed through decades of trying to set boundaries that only left me feeling abandoned and alone, before ultimately leading me to create this unique and transformative framework to build meaningful relationships.

Growing up, I was almost always alone. I have a younger brother and sister, but we rarely hung out together. They've almost always done their best to distance themselves from me so they could try to make friends despite the social disaster that my life had been. One summer, when our mom went to the UK for a month, I stayed at a neighbor's house while my brother and sister went to live with an aunt a few hours away. When we reunited at the end of summer, I remember being quite jealous of the stories they told of all the fun they had together and the friends they made at our aunt's place.

In school, I was a reject even among other rejects. I rarely had a friend. I played alone, ate alone, did my school work alone, and even dreamed alone. I would often play by myself on the fringes of the school grounds to avoid the attention of the kids who would bully me several times a day. I couldn't understand why the other kids would rather pick on me than play with me. My mom kept me home from school one day. I don't remember why she did, but I do remember being excited because I got to go to the playground knowing there would be no one else there to pick on me. I was elbows deep into digging tunnels in the sand when suddenly, a preschooler in the neighborhood took exception to what I was doing and started hitting me. I didn't understand what I'd done to deserve this treatment, so I ran home and hid in my room for the rest of the day.

Those rare occasions I did have friends, we didn't actually have much in common, other than both being outcasts. We were each so desperate to have a friend that we would hang out together and pretend we liked whatever the other person liked. I pretended I had a passion for cars so I could be friends with someone whose family lived in a junk yard. I enjoyed hearing them talk about all the things they knew about cars that most adults couldn't comprehend. To this day, because of that friendship, I still have an interest in cars that I've never pursued. I smoothly transitioned into becoming a chameleon. I would become whatever I needed to be in order to make a friend. It didn't work very often, but as I got older, I got better at it. In high school I adopted a 'country' persona when I found out a girl I was interested in (another outcast like me) liked country music. She was just as lonely as I was and it worked. We dated for a while until we tried to get to know each other better. It turned out we didn't actually have much at all in common.

As I transitioned into adulthood, this 'people-pleasing' did manage to fix some of my loneliness more often than it had in school. I took on the persona of the people I found myself around. One year I was the 'party host' that always had a place where my 'friends,' often people I didn't even know, could go to sleep off their hang-over or escape their parents' tyranny. Another year I was the head-banger, I grew my hair out (it's still long today) and started listening to heavy metal, a very 80's thing to do. I even took on the persona of 'nanny' at one point so I could have a safe place to live and some built-in friends. In the end, I was still lonely because none of these persona's attracted anyone to get to know the real me.

When I shared my people pleasing habits and continued loneliness with people I knew that I thought could help me, including my therapist, they all said the same thing: "You need to set better boundaries." I read the Boundaries book by Henry Cloud and John Townsend with growing hope. I learned what I could about boundaries and started setting them with the people in my life yearning for the authentic relationships promised in the book. I told my headbanger friends that I also liked country ... and classical music, as well as pop, rap, and dance music. In fact, a lot of the metal music they were listening to I found repetitive and boring. I told the lady I was nannying for that I wanted to pursue a relationship with a girl I had just met. I told my D&D (Dungeons and Dragons) group that I would be spending less time preparing for our game sessions because I wanted to spent some time with this girl I had just met. I was quickly reminded why I became a people pleaser in the first place. When I set boundaries with the people in my life, most of the time they would choose to exit my life rather than honor my boundaries. I don't have any metalhead friends anymore. The lady I was nannying for kicked me out and ghosted me. And almost all of my D&D friends stopped talking to me as well. It felt like I had put a toll booth on the bridge that connected me to them, and they chose to sacrifice our friendship rather than pay the toll. I was alone again ...

except for the girl I had just met.

I remember the night we met like it was yesterday. It was one of the happiest moments of my life. We were at a party. I was not flirting with her like nearly every other guy at the party was. I was too scared. Every girl I had ever been interested in had eventually rejected me. Most of them even before I told them I was interested. The couple girls I had dated by this time dumped me when they discovered the people pleaser they started dating was a façade. I wasn't going to make that mistake again. So when this new girl fought off the attention of the other guys long enough to sit down beside me and tell me she was interested in me, my very drunk brain fell back onto the only other personality trait I'd ever tried: arrogance. I told her I was also interested, while trying not to seem too interested. Somehow that worked.

But I still had no idea who I was. Over the next few years, we dated, had a couple kids, and got married. I quickly slid back into my people pleasing habits, which didn't have the expected result. We fought, a lot. I tried the arrogance that seemed to attract her to me in the first place. That made things even worse. I even tried using these boundaries I'd read about a while back. While she didn't exactly leave me since we had kids together, setting boundaries with her still didn't give me the fulfilling relationship I'd read about in the book. I continued the cycle of people pleasing -> setting boundaries -> feeling rejected and alone -> people pleasing. Then, one day she left. And I was alone again. Same result as before. Nothing I had tried had worked. I'd poured everything I had and everything I was into that relationship, and it was over. How could it have happened any other way? She couldn't connect with the real me. How could she when I couldn't even connect with the real me. I didn't know who I was.

Thus began the start of my evolution into Unconditional Boundaries. After she left, I spent several years battling depression and trying to figure out who I really am. As I learned more about myself, and shared what I learned with others, two things happened. First, almost all of the people in my life drifted away. Although this hurt at first, I realized it didn't hurt as much as feeling lonely around them. Second, I gradually started meeting, and connecting, with people who shared some of my true values. Most of the people in our church outright rejected me when my wife left, but one didn't. He and I had a couple heart-felt conversations. He was going through some major changes in his life and family too.

I eventually dated someone else as I tried to figure out who I was. This time I tried to let her see the real me. She seemed to like that. I'd tell her something about myself. She'd either like it or ignore it. No fighting. As we got to know each other better, there were more things we liked about each other, but there were also more things we didn't like about each other. I found myself slowly slipping back into people pleasing. That's when she recognized this wasn't going to work for either of us and broke it off. But I had learned something I'd never known before. Being myself had allowed her to connect with me on her terms. She could decide if she liked the real me or not, and the kicker was, for the most part she DID like the real me. Sure there were a couple characteristics she couldn't live with, but that's what dating is supposed to be for, to figure out if we're compatible enough to spend our lives together. We aren't, but that isn't anyone's fault. It's simply an indication that we have some key differences in our core values. This was a critical revelation for me.

I started using this perspective with other people in my life. I started comparing their values with mine, then assessing the importance of the values we share versus the importance of the values we didn't share. I discovered something amazing. I could make friends with people with whom I shared some values … even if some of our core values were different. The more important the values are to each of us that we share, the deeper the friendship. On the flip side. If instead our most core values are different, we'd benefit from keeping our friendship shallow. In this way, I've been able to create friendships almost out of thin air.

Today I have a few very close friends and a variety of friends of varying depth and shared interests. For almost any thought or idea I have, there is someone I can share it with and find a truly authentic connection. This, my friends, is what real connection, real friendship, and true love and happiness feels like. In this book, I hope to show you too how to have what I have: true belonging.

CHAPTER ONE

The Limitations of Traditional Boundaries

Sophia took a deep breath before dialing her sister's number. Her sister Amanda often offered unsolicited advice, and it was starting to get on Sophia's nerves. She planned to give Amanda an ultimatum— either stop giving unsolicited advice or Sophia would no longer confide in her.

Sophia's impulse represents a common use of traditional boundaries. When someone's behavior bothers us, the go-to response is to set expectations and reduce contact if those expectations aren't met. These consequences usually involve avoiding them or completely cutting contact with them altogether. Many people also use criticism, blaming, or some kind of punishment like taking something they want away from them. And herein lies one of the core problems with the way most people set boundaries:

Consequences damage relationships.

The consequences enacted by traditional boundaries often end up dismantling the very relationships they aimed to improve. This is because the usual penalties—less contact, cutoff, criticism, and blaming—are inherently damaging.

For instance, Sophia's threat to stop confiding in Amanda might get Amanda to give less advice, or it might not. Either way it degrades their sisterly bond. Sophia loses emotional intimacy with Amanda and damages their ability to connect on a deep level.

When our goals are to improve relationships, traditional boundaries often backfire. Their consequences can create resentment and degrade the connection, rather than bringing them closer. They often lead to giving up on relationships that could have brought joy and fulfillment.

Unconditional Boundaries avoid this issue by focusing on building mutual understanding based on the values we share, not enacting consequences for the values we don't.

The second problem with traditional boundaries is their focus on trying to change others

The other core limitation is that traditional boundaries seek to change others' values and behavior to match our own. The emphasis is on conformity not connection.

For example, Sophia is trying to make Amanda align with her value of not wanting unsolicited advice. If she doesn't, she threatens to reduce contact with her sister. Sophia sees Amanda's different perspective as wrong, to be corrected with threats and consequences.

But not everyone shares our beliefs and desires. Humans have diverse, nuanced values. While we can assert our own boundaries, we cannot expect others to conform without damaging the relationship.

Unconditional Boundaries acknowledge this complexity. Instead of demands for change, the focus shifts to identifying areas of shared values to build the relationship positively.

Rather than threaten Amanda over the advice issue, Sophia could highlight something they both value . Their bond can be nurtured through those areas where their values align.

In summary, traditional boundaries often harm relationships and connections through their use of consequences. They also fail to recognize the nuances of differing human values by expecting conformity.

Unconditional Boundaries offer a more holistic approach to improve understanding while nurturing alignment and respecting differences. Let's look at more of Sophia's experiences with setting traditional boundaries in the next chapter.

CHAPTER TWO

Meet Sophia: One Woman Sets Traditional Boundaries

After learning about the benefits of boundaries and how they could change how people treated her, Sophia decided to use them to strengthen her relationships. She read several books on boundaries and did some online research including watching videos from people who had the kinds of relationships she wanted in her life.

First, she addressed the issue with her boyfriend Robert often prioritizing his friends on weekends rather than spending time with her. Sophia told Robert that going forward, he needed to keep his weekend evenings free for her and their relationship. She made it clear that if he continued choosing his friends over her, she would end their relationship since she refused to come second to his friends.

At first, Robert agreed to Sophia's expectations, not wanting to lose her. He declined invitations from his friends and made sure to be available when Sophia asked him out on weekends. However, this change did not last long. The romantic dates gave way to watching movies at his place, often ones he didn't enjoy. Robert began to resent Sophia controlling his social life. He started playing video games with his friends in the evenings when Sophia was watching a movie he wasn't interested in. They eventually bonded less and ended up just staying home each doing their own thing instead of either of them doing what they wanted to: spending time together and growing their relationship. Their intimacy suffered and they drifted apart.

What had started as Sophia standing up for her needs turned into an expectation that pushed Robert away.

Next, Sophia addressed the issue of her assistant Sara needing her direct input on nearly everything Sara did. Sara constantly sought validation from Sophia, seeking guidance on almost everything and asking if she was doing a good job. Sophia told Sara that she needed to start doing things on her own. She made it clear Sara would have to learn to be more independent, and stop coming to Sophia with every task or problem.

Sara was hurt by Sophia's disregard for her insecurity. She became anxious and unsure of herself, triple-checking everything and seeking affirmation from others instead of Sophia. Without compassion and understanding from her boss, Sara's confidence cratered. Her work suffered as she second-guessed her decisions. Sophia's insensitive boundary had made the situation worse rather than improving it.

Finally, Sophia decided to address the issue of her mother frequently stopping by unannounced. Sophia told her mother she wouldn't put up with surprise visits, so she was instituting a new rule - no more dropping by without calling first and asking if it was a good time. If her mother dropped by without calling first, Sophia said she would not let her in the house.

Sophia's mom Often forgot this rule until she was on her way to Sophia's house. After being refused entry a few times, she simply stopped dropping by at all unless Sophia invited her. She felt hurt and shut out by Sophia's rigid approach. The spontaneous visits had been an expression of her love and her attempt to stay connected to her daughter. The demanding, inflexible boundary damaged their once close relationship. Her mother no longer felt connected to her daughter and soon fell into loneliness and depression.

In all cases, Sophia's traditional boundaries focused on the other person, asking them to change, and distancing herself from them if they didn't comply. However, this approach based on consequences and conformity ended up straining her relationships rather than strengthening them.

Sophia realized that boundaries rooted in expectations and consequences that distance her from those she cared about couldn't create the depth of connection and fulfilling relationships she truly craved. She wanted a different approach - one focused on sharing values instead of navigating differences.

Sophia discovered the concept of unconditional boundaries. By letting go of trying to change others and enforcing rules, and instead connecting through shared values, she realized she could build bridges that joined her to people who shared her values. Her relationships could deepen through shared goals and vulnerability, providing the path to bypass their differences.

CHAPTER THREE

Unveiling Unconditional Boundaries

As humans, we are social creatures, striving for connections that bring joy, understanding, and a sense of belonging. Yet, we also crave autonomy, respect, and personal space - a need for delineation between 'self' and 'others.' This delineation is what we call 'personal boundaries.' Traditionally, these boundaries are lines drawn in the sand, defining where one person ends, and another begins.

Traditional boundaries are designed to protect us, to act as shields against harmful influences and preserve our individuality. They allow us to express our needs and desires, say 'no' when necessary, and keep our personal life from becoming a free-for-all. Yet, this traditional approach to boundaries, with its focus on differentiating 'me' from 'everyone else,' has significant shortcomings. It fails to foster the meaningful connections we yearn for, creating an invisible wall that often separates us from others, leaving us feeling isolated and disconnected.

Enter 'Unconditional Boundaries,' a revolutionary approach to personal boundaries that transcends the rigidity of traditional definitions. This concept introduces two types of boundaries - 'Bridges' and 'Barriers.' They emerged from a need for a better approach that encourages connection with those who align with our values and protects us from those who don't.

'Bridges' are a way of sharing our desires, preferences, and values to invite others into our world. When we build bridges, we provide an open invitation to those who resonate with our values to connect with us on a deeper level. These bridges serve to guide people towards us, illuminating the path to a connection that provides us our deepest desires: love and fulfillment. On the flip side, well-defined bridges also offer clarity to those who do not share our values, signaling that our paths may not intersect harmoniously.

However, not everyone who walks across our bridge will respect our wellbeing. Some may choose to connect with us without respecting our values. In such cases, our bridges must evolve into 'Barriers.'

'Barriers' serve as the protective walls we traditionally associate with personal boundaries. They ensure we maintain a necessary distance from those who do not share our values or respect our personal space. Barriers help us to navigate our social landscapes without compromising our emotional well-being or sacrificing our personal integrity.

The introduction of Bridges and Barriers within Unconditional Boundaries encourages us to consciously choose our relationships. It urges us to focus on building meaningful connections with those who resonate with our values and keep a healthy distance from those who don't. Instead of merely serving as a protective mechanism, boundaries become a tool to cultivate deeper, more rewarding relationships.

This book is your journey towards mastering Unconditional Boundaries. You'll explore the depths of 'Bridges' and 'Barriers,' learning to implement them effectively in various scenarios. With the framework of Unconditional Boundaries, you'll navigate through life's complex web of relationships, enhancing the connections that enrich you and distancing those that drain you.

In the next chapter, we'll delve deeper into the concept of 'Bridges' – what they are and their role in fostering meaningful connections. We'll accompany Sophia as she takes her first steps towards building bridges, inviting us to witness the transformation that Unconditional Boundaries can bring about.

CHAPTER FOUR

Building Bridges - A Journey to Deeper Connections

Bridges, in the world of Unconditional Boundaries, are gateways to deeper connections. They are an open invitation, showcasing our desires, preferences, and values to others, allowing them to understand who we are and what we seek in our relationships. They are the lampposts that guide people to the gates in our walls and highlight the signs that describe what they can find when they cross the threshold into our lives. They also provide clear signals to those whose values might not align with ours, subtly guiding them to seek connections elsewhere.

Sophia, our protagonist, yearned for such deep, meaningful connections in her life. Her busy schedule, filled with work commitments and family responsibilities, often left her feeling stretched thin, her relationships strained and unfulfilling. She longed for a balance, a harmony of expectations that would allow her to nurture her relationships without losing herself in the process. Bridges, she hoped, would be her pathway towards achieving this.

Sophia decided to start this journey with the man she loved - Robert. Their relationship was warm, understanding, and full of shared laughter. Yet, Sophia longed for more. She wished for them to spend more quality time together, to share experiences that would help them grow as a couple. As she broached this subject, she used her bridge, expressing her desire for a regular date night each week, a ritual just for them. Robert, a man whose values aligned closely with hers, was receptive to her request, his smile a tacit acceptance of the invitation extended.

With her first successful bridge built, Sophia turned her attention to her work. David, a junior member of her team, often sought her guidance, consuming a substantial portion of her time. While she appreciated his eagerness to learn, Sophia wished for him to try a few things independently before reaching out to her. This was her next bridge - an invitation to David to consult the training materials or seek advice from coworkers before approaching her. David, whose values centered around teamwork and growth, appreciated Sophia's gentle nudge towards self-reliance and responded positively.

Next was Sophia's family, her support system, her stronghold. Sophia loved her sister, Amanda. Their conversations, however, often leaned heavily towards advice, leaving Sophia feeling unheard. Her next bridge was with Amanda. Sophia expressed her desire for conversations that were more about listening and less about providing solutions. Amanda, whose values were steeply rooted in helping those she cares about, took a moment to understand Sophia's perspective. Though initially surprised, she appreciated Sophia's honesty and offered find another way to help her sister rather than give her advice.

Building bridges was not as daunting as Sophia had feared. Instead of setting expectations, Sophia discovered that expressing her desires and preferences clearly increased rapport with people. She felt more connected to Robert, appreciated David's effort to become more independent, and looked forward to her next conversation with Amanda.

As Sophia reflected on her experiences, she realized that bridges were her tool for deeper, more rewarding connections. They allowed her to communicate her needs subtly yet effectively, enhancing the mutual understanding in her relationships. She also understood that bridges were not a guarantee of alignment but a beacon of her values, guiding those who resonated with them closer and letting others know it's okay to seek connection elsewhere.

As we continue to explore this transformative approach, the next step is an essential one: identifying our values. Only with a clear understanding of what truly matters to us can we build effective, authentic bridges. Stay tuned for the next chapter, where we delve into this pivotal aspect of Unconditional Boundaries, equipping ourselves with the knowledge to build clear, value-aligned bridges.

CHAPTER FIVE

Identifying Your Values

Walking through life without being aware of our values is like walking into an art gallery blindfolded. You know you're surrounded by artwork, each piece unique and evoking different feelings, but you're unable to appreciate any of it. Our values are the principles and beliefs that guide our actions, behaviors, and decisions, shaping the decisions we make in our lives.

Values are not about right or wrong. They are deeply personal, varying from person to person. They represent who we are, the essence of our being. Uncovering these values is a journey into self-awareness, an exploration that allows us to align with those who share our fundamental principles and helps us build bridges that facilitate meaningful connections.

To begin this journey of discovery, find a quiet space where you can introspect. Having someone trustworthy and understanding by your side to ask you, "What's important to you?" repeatedly can aid this process. Answer without censorship, without considering what might be 'expected' or 'right.' Keep answering until you feel you've unearthed enough values that you have a better understanding of yourself. You don't need an exhaustive list. What matters is uncovering those principles that truly resonate with your core self.

Once you have your list, take the time to rank these values based on their importance to you. This is a delicate exercise, one that requires honesty and introspection. The purpose is to understand not just what values you hold, but also their hierarchy in your life. It's a journey into understanding the motivations behind your actions, your reactions, and your decisions.

Remember, though, that conflicts in our life often arise from an internal conflict of values. For instance, consider someone enduring a toxic relationship. The abusive partner is solely responsible for their abusive behavior; they are the ones at fault. However, the person enduring the abuse might be dealing with an internal conflict between the desire to be loved and the need to feel safe. The abusive partner manipulates this internal conflict to their advantage, creating a cycle that seems impossible to break.

Similarly, when someone experiences conflicts with their boss at work, it might be because their values of transparency and teamwork are clashing internally with the value of financial security that their job provides. Their boss might take advantage of this internal conflict, leading to a toxic work environment.

These external manifestations of our internal conflict are never our fault. The person acting abusively or creating a toxic environment bears that responsibility. Being aware of our values and their hierarchy can offer us the clarity needed to see these situations for what they are. It can help us understand the internal dynamics at play, allowing us to regain control and find a path forward.

This journey into self-awareness isn't just about understanding ourselves better. It's about empowering ourselves, about finding solutions to external conflicts by resolving our internal ones. And by doing so, we can ensure that our bridges and barriers—our boundaries—are deeply rooted in our values.

In the next chapter, we will delve into the practical application of this newfound understanding of our values, guiding you on the journey of 'Building Bridges.' Let's explore how you can actively start incorporating your values into setting boundaries that enable deeper, more meaningful connections.

CHAPTER SIX

Building Bridges: A Step-by-Step Guide

Embarking on the journey to establish deeper connections can feel like navigating uncharted territory. Fear not, for this chapter will equip you with the map and tools necessary to construct your bridges effectively. Bridges, as you remember, are our invitations for others to align with our values, providing the chance for our relationships to flourish in newfound depths.

Choose your intended result

Begin with clarity in your intended result. The aim here is to be precise enough that those around you can understand what it is you're requesting. If the outcome you desire is clearer, the alignment or misalignment with your bridge will be more apparent to others. For instance, instead of stating, "I want more quality time with my partner," clarify with something like, "I want to establish a weekly date night."

Choose your responses to alignment

Next, equip yourself with responses for those who align with your bridge. Prepare at least one verbal and one non-verbal response. These responses should not only express your appreciation but also indicate the deepening connection. A verbal response could be something like, "I'm so happy we're doing this," followed by a non-verbal response that could be as intimate as a kiss - a universal sign of deepening romantic connection.

Choose your responses to misalignment

Now, let's focus on responses for when people's values don't align with your bridge. Your aim here is to convey understanding and acceptance of their differing values. Your verbal and non-verbal responses can display this acceptance, perhaps with a phrase such as, "I understand our interests may vary," accompanied by a non-verbal response such as a friendly nod.

Let's put this into perspective with Sophia's life. Sophia's intention was to spend more quality time with Robert, her boyfriend, by establishing a weekly date night. When Robert agreed, Sophia's happiness shone through her verbal response, "I'm thrilled we're doing this, Robert," followed by a non-verbal response - a heartfelt kiss.

Similarly, Sophia aimed to foster independence in David, a junior member of her team. She expressed her intent for him to attempt to find solutions independently before seeking her guidance. When David succeeded in resolving an issue on his own, she praised him with, "Well done, David. I knew you could figure it out," and an approving nod. Conversely, when David fell short or made a mistake, she reassured him by arranging for further training or by offering a coworker's assistance. This showed David that Sophia supported his growth and learning, despite the hurdles.

As we continue this exploration of boundaries, remember that building bridges is more than a strategy; it's a journey of personal growth and authenticity. The application of these principles will assist you in enhancing your connections with those around you.

In the next chapter, we're going to examine the application of bridges in a variety of relationships, especially those within the workplace. After all, the workplace, while often challenging, is a fertile ground for building and deepening relationships.

CHAPTER SEVEN

Building Bridges in Work Relationships

It is said that our work relationships can have as significant an impact on our wellbeing as our personal ones. In the workplace, where various personalities and priorities coexist, setting bridges to invite and nurture healthier, more productive relationships becomes an invaluable tool.

Consider the experiences of Sophia, an empathetic leader, skilled at cultivating strong work relationships using bridges. Let's examine her interactions with three key people in her professional life - Mike, the CEO; Jessica, a fellow project manager; and Sara, her assistant.

Sophia's intended result with Mike is to prompt him to hold weekly discussions concerning the realistic workload her team can handle within office hours. When Mike appreciates her suggestion and commits to this weekly alignment, Sophia responds warmly. She graces him with a genuine smile - a silent expression of relief and gratitude. Verbal appreciation follows, "Thank you, Mike, for understanding. This coordination will help us work more effectively and sustainably."

However, not all interactions align with Sophia's desired result. If Mike overlooks Sophia's request, she doesn't react with resentment or defeat. Instead, she accepts Mike's differing value - his pursuit of maximizing productivity. She maintains composure, articulating her concerns calmly, "Mike, I understand that your objective is to maximize our productivity. Let's find a balance that helps us achieve high output without risking team burnout. Do you have suggestions on how we can best accomplish this?" Her open-handed gesture signifies her willingness to understand and negotiate a solution that suits them both.

With Jessica, a fellow project manager, Sophia wishes to be involved in decisions impacting her projects. When Jessica incorporates Sophia's suggestion and begins involving her in the decision-making process, Sophia acknowledges Jessica's effort, reciprocating with a thankful nod and a vocal expression of gratitude, "Thank you, Jessica. This collaborative decision-making process will indeed enhance the effectiveness of our projects."

In scenarios where Jessica overlooks her request and makes decisions independently, Sophia responds with understanding and persistence. "Jessica, I appreciate your efficiency and understand that you may find it quicker to make decisions independently. However, since these decisions significantly impact my projects, could we brainstorm a way for me to be more involved, while still maintaining the workflow you prefer?" Sophia's supportive nod emphasizes her openness to compromise and a shared solution.

In her relationship with Sara, Sophia wishes to empower Sara to troubleshoot on her own before seeking immediate assistance. When Sara shows initiative and begins resolving issues independently, Sophia makes it a point to recognize Sara's growth. She rewards her effort with an appreciative smile and a vocal recognition, "Sara, I noticed you've been tackling these challenges head-on. I'm proud of how far you've come."

Yet, when Sara continues to lean on Sophia for immediate help, Sophia fosters growth through gentle encouragement, "Sara, I admire your attention to detail and your desire to get things right. But I believe that you also have the capability to navigate these tasks. Could we devise a plan that gives you some time to troubleshoot on your own while ensuring you still feel supported?" Her encouraging smile speaks volumes, reflecting her unwavering confidence in Sara's capabilities.

Through these examples, it becomes clear that building bridges isn't about demanding change or forcing alignment. Instead, it's about expressing our values and inviting others to understand and align with them. It's about offering responses that foster deeper connections when they align and showing acceptance when they don't, emphasizing that differing values are just as valid as our own.

In our next chapter, we'll explore the application of bridges in personal relationships, taking a step further in our understanding of this new evolution of boundaries.

CHAPTER EIGHT

Building Bridges in Family Relationships

Every family has its unique dynamics, and each individual family member their personal perspectives. Establishing bridges in a family setting is essential to preserve harmony while respecting each person's values. Let's delve into Sophia's life to understand how she builds bridges within her family.

Sophia's father has a habit of being pessimistic about her career choices. Sophia wanted her father to support her career decisions or, at the very least, to remain neutral about them. She figured out a way to show him how much it meant to her. The next time her father shared a positive or neutral remark about her career, Sophia hugged him warmly, letting her action communicate her gratitude. Or she'd say, "Thanks, Dad. Your support means a lot to me." The feeling of being appreciated touched her father. Alternatively, she'd write him a heartfelt note, thanking him for his supportive words.

However, when her father reverted to his old habit of making pessimistic comments about her career, Sophia was ready. She turned to him and, with a look of genuine curiosity on her face, asked, "Dad, it seems like we see my career differently. Is there a way we can discuss my job in a way that respects both our perspectives?" Sophia's response showed her father that she wasn't trying to change his views but wanted to find a mutually respectful way to discuss their differing perspectives.

Sophia's mother, a lovely lady, had a habit of visiting her home without any prior notice. Sophia desired her mother to inform her before visiting. So when her mother called or texted her about a planned visit, Sophia responded with a warm smile and expressed her gratitude. "Thanks for letting me know, Mom. I look forward to your visit." However, if her mother didn't inform her and just dropped by, Sophia would give her a gentle look, expressing understanding, and say, "Mom, it seems we have different reasons for your visits. Can we talk about those differences and come up with something that works for both of us?" By suggesting a conversation about their differing expectations, Sophia opened a way for her and her mother to find a solution that honored both their needs.

Lastly, let's consider Sophia's sister, Amanda. Amanda had a tendency to offer unsolicited advice, which Sophia found intrusive. Sophia wanted Amanda to give advice only when asked. So, when Amanda refrained from offering unsolicited advice and waited for Sophia to ask, Sophia gave her a thumbs-up or thanked her verbally. However, if Amanda slipped into her old habit, Sophia would smile gently at her and say, "Amanda, it seems we have different thoughts on when advice should be shared. Can we discuss a system where I don't feel so bombarded with your suggestions and still give you a chance to share them with me?" Sophia's response indicated her willingness to respect Amanda's need to share advice while also seeking a method that worked for both of them.

Each of these examples demonstrates how Sophia built bridges with her family members. She was not demanding changes in their behavior. Instead, she expressed her needs and responded to their alignment or misalignment with understanding and respect, always aiming for a deeper connection or maintaining the current relationship.

In the next chapter, we'll discuss how to build bridges in intimate relationships, where the stakes might be high, and emotions often run deep. Stay tuned for an exploration of building bridges in the most personal spaces of our lives.

CHAPTER NINE

Building Bridges in Romantic Relationships

Just as the sun was disappearing behind the horizon, painting the sky with hues of orange, Sophia sat down on her patio, her laptop before her. A cup of jasmine tea on the side, she started musing about her relationship with Robert.

Sophia and Robert had a beautiful connection, punctuated with moments of profound intimacy and joy. Still, there were areas where she desired more harmony, more alignment. She knew that 'building bridges' in a romantic relationship could be challenging, but it was essential for creating a stronger bond. Sophia decided to start building bridges with Robert, focusing on three areas: Quality Time, Intimacy, and Resolving Conflict.

Sophia valued quality time in her relationship. She desired a weekly "date night" - a time they would carve out of their busy schedules exclusively for each other, free from all distractions. She wanted Robert to agree to this concept, where they could create memories together, whether that involved a candlelit dinner at their favorite restaurant, a cozy movie night in their living room, or simply a walk under the stars.

Sophia crafted her bridge, imagining a positive response from Robert: "That sounds wonderful, Sophia. I'd love to spend more quality time with you too." Her heart warmed at the idea. And if he embraced the concept, she'd respond with a smile and a tender kiss, signaling a deepening of their bond. If he did not, she'd hold his hand and say, "I understand if you need some time to think about it, but I'd love to hear any suggestions you have for us to spend more time together."

Physical affection was another realm Sophia wanted to emphasize in her relationship. She desired that they deliberately set aside time for physical intimacy each day - a goodnight kiss, a comforting hug in the morning, or "making love". She yearned for these gestures to become part of their daily routine.

If Robert showed enthusiasm for this idea, Sophia would respond with a long, enveloping hug, demonstrating the intimacy she wished to enhance. If his response was less encouraging, she'd reassure him by saying, "It's okay if you're unsure about this, Robert. I'd love to hear any thoughts you have about how we can increase our physical connection in a way that's comfortable for both of us."

Lastly, Sophia knew that no relationship was devoid of conflicts. It was how they chose to navigate these conflicts that mattered. Sophia wished to create a commitment with Robert: whenever a disagreement cropped up, they would consciously choose a time to discuss it, articulate the issue clearly, and engage in non-defensive listening and respectful conversation. She envisioned turn-taking in expressing feelings, utilizing "I" statements, and calling for a time-out if emotions ran high.

Upon Robert's acceptance of this idea, Sophia would gently squeeze his hand, a non-verbal acknowledgement of their deepening trust. If he disagreed, she would remain calm, responding with, "I understand, Robert. It's important to me that we find a way to manage conflicts that feel right for both of us. Do you have any suggestions?"

As Sophia finished detailing her bridges, she felt a sense of relief wash over her. She knew she was taking an essential step toward enhancing her relationship with Robert. She understood that these bridges might require adjustment and patience, but she was willing to cross that bridge when she came to it. After all, love was about connection, communication, and compromise.

In the next chapter, we'll dive into Barriers, the Unconditional Boundaries that protect us from hurtful or destructive relationships.

CHAPTER TEN

Barriers - Setting Boundaries that Protect

At times, even the most ardent bridge-builder may find themselves staring at a gulf too wide to span. This chapter invites you to navigate such terrain, the landscape where values diverge so much that their paths threaten your authenticity. Here we enter the realm of Barriers, protective measures that safeguard your identity and serenity from the potential storm of clashing values.

Barriers aren't walls of denial or avoidance; they're conscious decisions to prioritize your authenticity when facing significantly misaligned values. They operate under the principle of self-preservation without a mandate to alter the other person's values.

To illustrate this further, let's revisit Sophia's relationships, as introduced in Chapter 4.

Sophia had suggested a weekly date night with Robert, but what if he had outright rejected her invitation, saying he wanted all his evenings for other plans? Sophia would be faced with a stark divergence in their relationship values. In this case, she might set up a Barrier. This could manifest as a respectful conversation about how they both want something different from a relationship and a reevaluation of how much she can invest in a relationship lacking in mutual quality time. The Barrier isn't about changing Robert; it's about respecting her need for connection and shared experiences in a relationship.

In the realm of her professional life, Sophia wished for inclusion in decisions involving her projects. But what if Jessica had refused Sophia's request? Here, Sophia could establish a Barrier by reducing her reliance on Jessica's input for her projects and seeking collaborative opportunities elsewhere. Again, Sophia isn't seeking to change Jessica's work style. Instead, she's protecting her value for collaborative decision-making.

Sophia yearned for empathy from her sister, Amanda. However, suppose Amanda was reluctant to accommodate this. In this situation, Sophia could choose to engage with Amanda in a different way that doesn't require empathy from her sister, preserving her emotional wellbeing. This Barrier isn't about Sophia insisting Amanda change; it's about Sophia protecting her own emotional needs.

In each of these cases, Sophia's Barriers come into play when she realizes that the gap between her values and the values of others could affect her negatively. Through setting these Barriers, she has not only protected herself but also remained open to connecting with each of them in different ways.

Her interactions remain authentic and respectful, and yet she establishes a protective distance. The Barriers enable Sophia to remain true to her values, even when they significantly misalign with those of others in her life.

These examples showcase the power and respect derived from establishing Barriers. They allow us to not only protect our authentic selves but also honor the values of others without letting them overshadow our own. This ability to place protective boundaries around our core values enables us to navigate our relationships confidently and authentically.

To sum up, Barriers aren't about winning or changing others; they are about asserting and preserving our values in the face of significant misalignment. They allow us to maintain our authenticity, marking a respectful distance when necessary. As we journey forward, let's carry this knowledge into our relationships, shaping them with both the bridges we build and the barriers we set.

CHAPTER ELEVEN

Identifying Your Limits

You're like an architect of your life, designing and building the relationships you want to have with the people around you. But how do you make sure these relationships remain healthy and productive? It all comes down to understanding and respecting your limits. Let's dive into that in this chapter.

Have you ever watched a pair of dancers in a ballet or a salsa dance? The grace of their movement, the synchronicity in their steps —it's mesmerizing. That's the magic of alignment, and the same applies to our values in relationships. When we and the other person share common values, or at least have values that don't conflict, our interactions can become as graceful as a well-choreographed dance.

Like two dancers moving in sync, aligned values allow for a harmony that can lead to a beautiful relationship. However, it's essential to understand that alignment doesn't mean identicality. There can be variations in actions and perspectives, but as long as these variations don't contradict our core values, we're still dancing to the same rhythm. For instance, Sophia may value quality time with her boyfriend, and if he shows up for their date nights, even if sometimes late, they are still aligning on their value of quality time.

Imagine Sophia places great importance on continuous self-improvement and learning, while her friend values skill mastery.

Though not identical, these values can harmoniously exist side-by-side. Sophia's pursuit of learning can motivate her friend's desire for mastery, and her friend's focus on developing a deep understanding of a single skill can inspire Sophia to delve deeper into her areas of interest. Their mutual respect for personal growth and development, albeit approached differently, signifies the compatibility of their values. This harmony and mutual enhancement characterize the second limit of compatible values.

The first two limits fall within the realm of building bridges. Bridges connect us, fostering understanding and empathy, allowing for deeper, more meaningful relationships. They stand strong when our values align or are compatible, helping us cross any gaps in understanding or difference.

What happens when the dance falls out of sync? When the dancers' movements conflict and they step on each other's toes? That's what competitive values feel like. When our values start to contradict or clash, it becomes hard to keep the dance going. This is our third limit. Sophia and her co-worker might start having issues if her co-worker values competition over cooperation, and this constant rivalry could strain their working relationship.

At the far end of the spectrum lie subversive values. Imagine a dance where one dancer constantly undermines the other, endangering the performance and potentially causing harm. That's the danger of subversive values. They don't just misalign; they actively threaten our authenticity and even our identity. For example, if Sophia's partner refuses to respect her personal space despite repeated discussions, that's a clear sign of subversive values, potentially threatening Sophia's sense of self-respect and autonomy.

When the dance of values becomes a battlefield, we need to protect ourselves, and barriers become essential. They act as shields, keeping us safe when the misalignment of values becomes too significant to navigate without getting hurt. Barriers aren't meant to alienate people but to safeguard our mental and emotional wellbeing.

Identifying and understanding our limits in relationships is a journey. It requires introspection, honesty, and courage. But, as you start to become more comfortable with recognizing these limits, you'll find your relationships becoming more genuine, healthier, and fulfilling. This is the dance of life, and you have the power to choreograph your part in it.

CHAPTER TWELVE

Building Barriers: Step-by-Step Guide

The lighthouse stands tall on the rocky shoreline, a beacon of light cutting through the fog. Each sweep of its beacon warns passing vessels of the jagged coast, ensuring their safe passage. It is neither punitive nor malicious. Instead, it stands as a protector, much like the Barriers we erect to protect ourselves in relationships.

We've spent considerable time delving into the foundations of Barriers, understanding their purpose and identifying when they are necessary. Now, it's time we navigate the mechanics of building these Barriers step-by-step.

Deciding What Limit Was Breached

The inception of a Barrier is a breached limit. Recognizing this breach requires a deep, introspective understanding of our own values. Defining the value that the other party misaligns with is a crucial first step. Ask yourself, "Which of my values is being countered here?"

Next, identify the invitation that was refused. This can be a direct invitation you extended or a a request you made. Did you invite your partner to spend quality time together only to have them prioritize their interests instead?

Finally, ascertain if their value is competitive or subversive to your own. This is a pivotal point, as it defines the type of Barrier you erect. Competitive values, while in disagreement, can coexist to some extent. Subversive values, on the other hand, are harmful and necessitate stronger Barriers.

Choosing Your Responses to the Breach

Upon identifying a breach, how do you react? Deciding on a set of responses is pivotal. These responses are not about punishing disobedience or making them pay for what they did; they are protective measures, manifestations of your Barrier.

Your verbal response should succinctly indicate a reduction in connection. A simple phrase like, "It seems like our values are conflicting here, I need some space to process this," can suffice.

Next, decide on a non-verbal action that reinforces your verbal response. A gentle, yet firm, distance physically or digitally can serve as a powerful non-verbal cue.

You may also choose a third, optional response that reinforces your Barrier further. This could be avoiding shared activities for some time or refraining from engaging in deep, personal discussions.

For competitive values, maintaining a limited connection is often feasible. Remember, these are values that, while in disagreement, don't pose significant harm. However, for subversive values, limiting the connection as much as possible is recommended. This could mean ceasing communication entirely or distancing yourself emotionally and physically to a greater extent.

Like the sweeping beam of the lighthouse, your Barriers are your protection against the rocky shoals of incompatible or harmful values. As we close this chapter, remember that Barriers aren't punitive measures, but protective ones. They stand as testaments to our self-understanding, self-respect, and our determination to stay true to ourselves, even amidst the foggiest of relationships.

CHAPTER THIRTEEN

Building Barriers in Work Relationships

Workplaces, a hive of diverse personalities and disparate priorities, often present unique challenges for individuals attempting to maintain fruitful relationships while protecting their core values. In these scenarios, where bridges invite alignment, barriers act as protectors when significant misalignment of values persist, despite best efforts. Barriers allow us to uphold our values without falling prey to competing or subversive values.

Let's revisit Sophia's journey. Her aptitude for constructing bridges in professional relationships is commendable. However, she understands the critical need for barriers when alignment of values isn't feasible.

Sophia values sustainable productivity, and she invited Mike, the CEO, to deliberate on a realistic workload for her team weekly. Suppose Mike consistently overlooks her invitation, favoring a high-pressure productivity approach, leading to her team's exhaustion. In this situation, Sophia's barrier might involve her contemplating a role change or considering a different company that aligns better with her values. She communicates this consideration respectfully, indicating a potential reduction in connection due to the significant misalignment of values.

With Jessica, Sophia values collaboration. She extended an

invitation to be involved in decisions impacting her projects. Imagine if Jessica repeatedly makes unilateral decisions, dismissing Sophia's requests. In response, Sophia might need to erect a barrier to safeguard her values and her projects' success. She could consider partnering with other project managers who value collaboration, signaling a decrease in her connection with Jessica due to the competitive nature of their values.

In her relationship with Sara, her assistant, Sophia values initiative and self-reliance. If Sara continues to heavily rely on Sophia, ignoring her nudges towards independence, Sophia may need to set up a barrier. Her response could include looking for a replacement assistant who values self-reliance, signifying a reduction in her connection with Sara.

In each example, barriers in work relationships are not tools for punishment or coercion. Instead, they're protective mechanisms that guard us against values that might compete with or subvert ours. These boundaries enable healthier work relationships, letting us thrive amidst considerable value discrepancies.

As we delve further into the exploration of boundaries, our next chapters will apply these concepts in personal relationships. Continue reading to discover how Sophia employs barrier-building in her personal life, gaining insight into this new evolution of boundaries.

CHAPTER FOURTEEN

Building Barriers in Family Relationships

In the mosaic of human relationships, family connections are the tiles that hold a special place. Bound by blood and history, our interactions with family often carry an emotional weight that exceeds many other relationships. Sophia's journey with bridges has taught us the value of seeking alignment, but what happens when the values of our loved ones consistently miss the mark? Enter the necessity of barriers - the boundary-building tool that shields us from significant value misalignment.

Let's walk with Sophia as she navigates the complex dynamics of her family relationships, armed with her newfound understanding of barriers.

Sophia's father is persistently pessimistic about her career choices. She has made repeated attempts to construct a bridge, inviting him to be more supportive or at least neutral. However, if her father continues to display resistance to her requests, Sophia considers a different approach. Sophia decides to stop discussing her career with her father entirely. Her barrier, a protective mechanism, safeguards her emotional well-being from his persistent pessimism.

Sophia gently communicates her decision, "Dad, I've realized our conversations about my career often leave me feeling disheartened. I think it might be best for now if we discuss other aspects of our lives instead." This response is not a rejection of her father but a loving reinforcement of the boundary protecting her values and emotional well-being.

Sophia loves her mother dearly. However, her mother's habit of dropping by unannounced disrupts Sophia's routine and encroaches on her value of predictability and personal space. Despite her attempts to build a bridge by asking her mother to inform her before visiting, suppose her mother continues to overlook her requests. In that case, Sophia finds it necessary to erect a barrier.

Sophia conveys her decision in a respectful yet firm manner, "Mom, I need some level of predictability in my daily routine. If you drop by without notice, I may not be able to invite you in." This response shows Sophia's steadfast commitment to her values while still expressing her affection for her mother.

Sophia's relationship with Amanda, her sister, presents a different challenge. Amanda often gives unsolicited advice, a practice that Sophia finds intrusive. If Sophia's bridge-building efforts fail to create alignment in their values, Sophia erects a barrier. She decides to spend less time with Amanda, not as a punitive measure, but to protect her own values and autonomy.

She carefully explains her decision, "Amanda, I appreciate your concern and I know you mean well, but the frequent unsolicited advice often feels intrusive. I think it might be best for now if we limit our time together." This response affirms Sophia's affection for Amanda while also highlighting the value discrepancy that necessitates the barrier.

In each of these situations, Sophia uses barriers not as a weapon of isolation, but as a shield of preservation, protecting her values. Remember, erecting barriers in family relationships is not about pushing loved ones away but about guarding our emotional health and personal values.

In the next chapter, we delve into the world of intimate relationships. We will explore how Sophia builds barriers when her deepest emotional needs and personal values face potential compromise. Continue on this journey to learn how to protect your emotional and value-based boundaries in the most personal spaces of your life.

CHAPTER FIFTEEN

Building Barriers in Romantic Relationships

As the early morning light streamed through the bedroom window, Sophia lay awake, her thoughts ablaze. The man sleeping soundly next to her was Robert, her lover, her confidante, her friend. Yet, nestled in the tranquility of their shared silence, she couldn't help but ponder the complex, intricate fabric of their relationship. Despite the profound affection and warmth that cradled their bond, Sophia was beginning to realize that certain aspects of their relationship fell short of aligning with her deeply held values. In such instances, Sophia discerned the necessity of erecting barriers - delineations carved with quiet fortitude and firm resolve.

Sophia cherished quality time. She dreamt of a romance where every week held the promise of a date night, an evening of shared laughter and whispered words. Yet, Robert's constant dismissal of this idea was starting to chip away at her hope. Understanding that this was a core value she wasn't willing to relinquish, Sophia decided to establish a barrier. She consciously began reducing the amount of time she spent with Robert, channeling her energies into her personal pursuits. This was her way of subtly signaling that their paths were deviating - a symbol of the widening gap between their shared experiences.

Intimacy, with its gentle caress and comforting warmth, was a language that Sophia believed was paramount to a thriving romantic relationship. Yet, her yearning for consistent expressions of love met with a wall when it came to Robert. Despite her attempts to bridge this divide, his unresponsiveness left her with a deepening sense of disconnect. Unwilling to compromise on this core value, Sophia erected another barrier. She began to temper her expectations, reducing her requests for physical intimacy - an act of self-preservation against the cold winds of rejection.

Conflicts, for Sophia, were not about winning or losing. They were opportunities for growth, gateways to deeper understanding and mutual respect. But Robert's evasive maneuvers and reluctance to engage in meaningful dialogues left their issues unresolved. Recognizing this discord, Sophia imposed a barrier here too. She started showing less interest in advancing their relationship, a poignant reminder of the corrosive impact unresolved conflicts were having on their bond.

In each of these situations, Sophia's barriers were not walls of resentment or anger. They were her way of preserving her personal values, her way of asserting that she deserved a relationship that echoed her deepest convictions.

Building barriers in a romantic relationship is not an act of surrender but an affirmation of self-worth. It signals an awakening to the realization that the relationship may not be evolving into the deeply satisfying and mutually beneficial union we desire. It highlights the importance of alignment in core values between partners for a relationship to truly flourish. If we find ourselves constantly erecting barriers in crucial aspects of our relationship, it might be more beneficial to consider finding a partner who resonates more closely with our values.

Remember, investing energy and emotions into a relationship that falls short of fulfilling our deepest desires can be profoundly draining and unfulfilling. It's crucial to weigh the value of each relationship against the effort needed to maintain our values within it. Barriers serve as a reminder to stay true to ourselves, allowing us to navigate our relationships with authenticity and integrity.

CHAPTER SIXTEEN

The Essence of Unconditional Boundaries

As we reach the end of our exploration into the world of Unconditional Boundaries, let's reflect on the depth and breadth of the journey we've embarked upon. This framework isn't just about setting boundaries; it changes our approach to building relationships, ultimately reshaping our lives.

Bridges have emerged as the cornerstone of our journey. They are the boundaries that embody our innermost values, desires, and aspirations. Through bridges, we express who we are and invite others to understand and connect with our authentic selves. These bridges are built on the foundation of shared values, illuminating paths towards deeper, more meaningful relationships. They are powerful expressions of our identity, showcasing what we believe and what we seek in others. By building bridges, we attract like-minded individuals and highlight to those whose values don't align with ours that they'd find better relationships with someone else.

In contrast to bridges, barriers are the boundaries that safeguard our core values. Instead of insisting they face punishment or consequences, Barriers allow us to distance ourselves from the people whose values clash with our own. They help us maintain our emotional and mental integrity in the face of discordant or harmful relationships. It's crucial to understand that barriers create space between people with incompatible values without judging those values as right or wrong, good or bad. They empower us to distance ourselves from situations that don't align with our values, to honor our beliefs, and to navigate our social landscapes as our authentic selves.

The journey of Unconditional Boundaries is deeply rooted in the understanding and acceptance of the diverse spectrum of human values. This framework challenges us to move beyond the traditional notion of boundaries, which often demands conformity and can lead to conflict, and instead embrace a more holistic approach. It's about recognizing that every individual has their unique set of values and that these values deserve respect and understanding. This recognition allows us to build bridges where there is alignment and set barriers where there is discord, all while building integrity in our relationships and ourselves.

Relationships, like life, are dynamic and ever-evolving. The Unconditional Boundaries framework guides us through this ever-changing landscape, offering tools and insights to navigate the complexities of human interactions. It teaches us to be adaptable, to reassess our values and boundaries as we grow and change. It encourages us to continually learn about ourselves and others, to adapt our bridges and barriers as needed, and to embrace the ebb and flow of connections in our lives.

As we conclude this journey, remember that the practice of Unconditional Boundaries is a lifelong endeavor. It requires continuous introspection. This framework isn't just about improving our relationships; it's about enhancing our overall well-being, fostering a deeper understanding of ourselves and others, and cultivating a life rich in authentic connections. Embrace this journey with an open heart, a willing mind, and the resolve to build bridges and set barriers that honor your true self.

As you move forward, carry with you the lessons and insights from this journey. Let them guide you in building a life filled with meaningful relationships, grounded in the beauty of your values and the strength of your authenticity. Unconditional Boundaries are a way of living, a path to a more connected, fulfilled, and authentic life.

Notes

Thank you for reading my book. I hope it helps you have better, more fulfilling relationships.

Here are the places you can find me and more of my content as well as further discussions about Unconditional Boundaries:

My YouTube Channel: Unconditional Boundaries
   My Podcast: Search for Unconditional Boundaries on Spotify, Apple Podcasts, and most other podcast platforms

You can email me at andy@unconditionalcoach.com

www.ingramcontent.com/pod-product-compliance
Lightning Source LLC
Chambersburg PA
CBHW060522280326
41933CB00014B/3074